Fearless Em

Build Emotional Resilience

Learn to Detach, Stop Over-Thinking, Master Your Emotions, and Bounce Back Effortlessly to Thrive in a Chaotic Environment

Devi Sunny

GRAB YOUR FREE GIFT BOOK

MBTI enumerates 16 types of people in the world. Each of us is endowed with different talents, which prove to be the innate strength of our personality. To understand the deeper psychology of your personality type, unique cognitive functions, and integrated personality growth path, visit www.clearcareer.in for a free download –

"Your Personality Strength Report"

Fearless Empathy Series

1) Book 1
   Set Smart Boundaries
2) Book 2
   Master Mindful No
3) Book 3
   Conquer Key Conflicts

Clear Career Inclusive Series

Book 1: _Raising Your Rare Personality_ is about understanding MBTI Personality types and their Ideal Careers, focusing on Rare Personality Types.

Book 2: _Upgrade as Futuristic Empaths_ is for those who want to understand how Empathy can be developed as a strength and discusses five steps to build a profile for successful careers.

Book 3: _Onboard as Inclusive Leaders_ helps to develop the essential qualities required for an inclusive leader, understand unconscious biases, the importance of psychological safety, and how it impacts workplace productivity.

Contents

About the Book 5

Introduction 7

1. Understanding Emotional Resilience 13

2. Struggles with Emotional Imbalance 24

3. Merits of Emotional Independence 33

4. Becoming Intelligent with Emotions 45

5. Developing Emotional Agility 56

6. Reinforce Healthy Emotions 67

Conclusion 80

About the Author 82

May I ask for a Review 83

Preview of Previous Books 84

Acknowledgement 98

References 100

About the Book

Every book hopes to find the right reader, someone who, like me, craves clarity and answers to the mysterious ways of life and how to navigate each step. Some of the insights discussed here may be familiar to you. Expertise comes with experience, but being aware and knowledgeable of the many aspects of our surroundings helps us recognize the situations and circumstances we find ourselves in. Let's face it; human beings are emotional creatures. It is because we have evolved cognitively. When our expectations or desires clash with reality, we often experience negative emotions. Sadness creeps in when things fall short of what we hoped for, while happiness takes over when they exceed our expectations. What is fascinating is that our thoughts are the triggers for these emotions. Exposing ourselves to new thoughts and environments can gradually bring about a shift in our feelings. We do know that our universe is constantly in motion. It is continually expanding and supporting growth. Growth implies change; thus, growth can encounter resistance. Sorrow can be an expression of unwillingness to accept reality or of a missed opportunity. Happiness, on the other hand, arises when everything is in alignment. Like any moving object that experiences wear and tear during its life, we also experience ups and downs. You've probably seen how asteroids burn and reduce in size due to the friction of Earth's atmosphere before landing on its surface. It is a universal law that everything in motion must follow an orbit, and as long as the object stays in alignment with its orbit, it has a natural end. However, when it deviates from its path, it wreaks havoc. As beings, do we also have a trajectory to follow? Our minds are limited to thinking based on our knowledge, so we need external inputs to fuel our thoughts. The information gathered through our five senses gets processed, and the output can be creative or destructive. Some minds are compassionate, where input falls onto a delicate internal canvas, leaving a profound impact. Because such minds feel deeply, they attach great importance to what they receive compared to others. What's important to understand is the investment of time and effort into what matters to you at any point in your life. Ask yourself if the benefit of your investment will stay with you forever. Investing in yourself—your knowledge and skills—will genuinely save you. The faster we realign with our intended orbit, the easier to predict success. Emotional resilience is the key to returning to your orbit swiftly. In the following pages, we'll explore practical ways to build emotional resilience. We'll discover strategies to bounce back from setbacks, adapt to change, and find balance amidst life's challenges. Remember, we are all on this journey together. Let's navigate the mysteries of life and build emotional resilience hand in hand.

Introduction

"Do external things distract you? Then make time for yourself to learn something worthwhile; stop letting yourself be pulled in all directions. But make sure you guard against the other kind of confusion. People who labor all their lives but have no purpose to direct every thought and impulse toward are wasting their time — even when hard at work."- Marcus Aurelius.

Imagine the costliest thing you own. It can be your phone, vehicle key, wallet, PIN, or room or house keys. Where would you have kept it safely? Wherever you store it, will you give its access to others? No. You would prefer to keep it with you. What would happen if you trust it with others? That entails a risk. What if you own a treasure you can't retain, no matter how you try, unless you use it?

"Time is the most precious element of human existence. The successful person knows how to put energy into time and how to draw success from time." - **Denis Waitley.**
Do you agree? We all have heard that time is the most precious thing we have. But have you realized how? What if I say it's not time itself, but the mind that uses time correctly that is the most precious thing we have? We all have healthy, working minds. Aren't we wealthy, then? So,

who is to blame if we cannot use our time correctly? Ourselves? Our minds? Do you agree that if we can use our minds properly, we can make the most available time? If you decide that your mind is a treasure, should it be kept aside safely? Will you make your mind accessible to others, particularly outsiders? Do you have the keys to your emotions?

We are all on a journey from birth to death. Have you seen anyone walking with another all the way unless they are Siamese twins? There might also be profound conflicts in the directions they should be moving. Unlike them, we will have different people joining us at various stages of life, starting with our parents, teachers, friends, siblings, family, classmates, soulmates, and whoever you would like to name. As you move forward, people may change if you are not bound by laws or a common purpose supporting mutual growth. It is a fact that the people in your life all have to leave you at some point; no one can walk with you until death in normal conditions.

Have you seen trees attacked by parasitic plants and termites? Some of them even have the potential to kill the tree. But trees can't help but coexist. Evolution enables us to move, think, express, act, and speak out. We know we need a healthy environment to sustain. We are careful about whom we let into our life and share our time with. We are products of our environment. It is because what we see and hear invokes thoughts in us, leading to actions. The inputs from all our five sensory senses lead to the ideas we entertain, triggering emotions and eventually influencing our actions.

You agree that your thoughts are constantly changing. So, similar to our thoughts, our emotions are akin to clouds. We have observed that they pass by, leaving a clear sky. Each person is responsible for managing their feelings individually by not using others or holding others accountable. Otherwise, our emotions will trap us in situations and with people, leaving us struggling to escape. Just as we move on from situations in life, our thoughts and emotions also move on. But we choose to engage in actions heavily relying on our current emotions, thinking that the benefits of these actions are permanent. In that case, we might be disappointed as the source of the feelings is always temporary.

"Your emotions are slaves to your thoughts. And you are a slave to your emotions." - **Elizabeth Gilbert.**

We evolved as humans because of our ability to think. Emotions are the byproducts of our thoughts. Are you aware of people who struggle to process their emotions? Negative emotions reduce productivity. To an extent, intuitive feelers or empaths need emotional resilience for integrated personality growth. We already possess basic physical features to survive: two eyes to see, a nose to breathe, and a mouth to eat. So, the majority of the human population is thus physically self-sufficient. However, we need to be complete emotionally and intellectually. We search for these remnants in others to make us whole; it is an energy exchange we seek. It is tough to sustain ourselves with an external energy source. But what is interesting is we can be self-sufficient intellectually and emotionally as well. It is possible to grow your mindset toward this goal by not depending on others to fulfill it; we have to nourish our minds as we feed our physical bodies.

Consider the resilience of our ancestors, who faced frequent child losses amidst ceaseless physical demands. Unlike today, emotional turmoil had to yield to urgent survival needs—evading wild threats and rival incursions. Swiftly adapting, they didn't dwell on emotional scars. Those with spare moments embraced healing arts, nurturing a balance between survival and tending to their hearts. In the film 'The Starling,' two couples mirror this blend, with the husband's honesty about depression driving therapy that includes the healing power of art. The wife's empathy for an injured bird becomes her source of solace. Their emotional evolution parallels the lessons of bygone eras, emphasizing compassion, emotional honesty, and growth amidst grief.

"But there was no need to be ashamed of tears, for tears bore witness that a man had the greatest courage, the courage to suffer." - **Viktor E. Frankl.**

With solutions for everything, thanks to the advancements in the modern age, life is made easy for us. So, there should also be hacks to overcome emotional turbulence. Ignorance of this skill would lead to unnecessary turmoil, tensions, loss of time, and even tragedies and pain. It is like a muscle that needs to be developed over time, and like any skill that requires time, patience, and experience to be fit, emotional resilience also needs to be learned and exercised. This book will delve deep into the psychology and science of emotional resilience. The following chapters will examine the 5Ws and 1H of Emotional Resilience.

This book is for those struggling with unexpressed anger, unseen tears, unsaid pain, and underestimated emotional struggles you go through. Life is designed to be tough so that the toughest wins the race. Consider it a game where you encounter even more challenging levels as you cross the previous ones. While there is no guarantee to reduce the intensity of the struggles you will face, if you can understand any meaning from your struggles, you may find it easier to sail through. We cannot predict future situations; they will differ for each of you. But a general direction of action will safeguard your interests in any case.

"A man who becomes conscious of the responsibility he bears toward a human being who affectionately waits for him or to an unfinished work will never be able to throw away his life. He knows the 'why' for his existence and will be able to bear almost any 'how'." - **Viktor E. Frankl.**

I have come across people who have had tough challenges. Why is it that they didn't give up? They must have had a reason, however undefinable; they just continued. Maybe they were bold enough to face these challenges or afraid to take their life. Or it could be that they had people to support them. But one thing is clear: if a tree has to grow and bear fruit, it has to survive all climates, adapt and yield; otherwise, the tree's life will end. We all have a choice to adjust and produce fruit. But why do you choose to live? Through their struggles, many have connected the dots backward to get a beautiful plan for their life; it had meaning, which they shared with others. We choose to quit because we think our struggles are the biggest. But when we realize it is not, we feel small and cowardly. The word "yield" has multiple meanings. Life will yield us so that we yield right. Big or small, you will be tested for your strength. Just as immunity is to your physical health, so is resilience to your emotional health. You work out at the gym or eat healthily to look good. But how fit is your inner self? How strong are you emotionally? Let's find out. Join me for your mental gym tour in the upcoming chapters.

1. Understanding Emotional Resilience

"Rather than being your thoughts and emotions, be the awareness behind them."- Eckhart Tolle.

In one of the recent Netflix Special, Comedian Chris Rock opened up about the unforgettable incident at the Oscars where Will Smith slapped him. Rock clarified that he didn't consider himself a victim and shared why he didn't retaliate during the incident. The whole thing started when Rock joked about Jada Pinkett Smith's hair loss condition, Alopecia. In response, Smith slapped Rock live on TV. When questioned about his lack of reaction, Rock humorously explained that his parents had taught him not to fight in front of white people, showing he was raised with a different approach to handling conflicts. The comedian asserted that he refuses to play the victim card and won't shed tears on talk shows like Oprah. With a touch of humor, he likened his resilience to that of boxer Manny Pacquiao, demonstrating that he took the slap like a champ.

Imagine ourselves in Chris Rock's place. Would we have the same attitude when insulted in public? How would we react? Whatever your answer, let's agree that it's not easy to deal with. Was his understanding or passive nature keeping him calm in the situation?

"The nearer a man comes to a calm mind, the closer he is to strength. You have power over your mind, not outside events. Realize this, and you will find strength." - **Marcus Aurelius.**

Emotional Resilience

Emotional resilience is your ability to remain stable and function usually, i.e., maintain your mental stability, regardless of external factors. It can be measured by how quickly you return to your normal functioning after traumatic situations. It can also be explained as your ability to recover quickly from difficult situations. Emotional Resilience can be developed. It is also the result of good willpower and self-discipline. Just as a triumph over a mountain climb starts with a single step, practice will take us closer to our highest potential. So, while knowing the methods to gain resilience is helpful, practical experiences are necessary to become experts. However, certain aspects like age, exposure to trauma, and gender are said to influence its development.

Emotional Intelligence Vs. Emotional Resilience

You can refer to Wikipedia's definition of Emotions as the mental state brought on by neuro-physical changes associated with thoughts, feelings, behavioral responses, and a degree of pleasure or displeasure. Emotional Intelligence is the skill to perceive, use, understand, manage, and handle emotions. People with EQ can recognize their own emotions and those of others. They can use this information to guide their thinking, differentiate feelings, and adjust emotions to adapt to situations. Hence, you will see that emotional intelligence is the foundation on which resilience can be built. Emotional resilience is effective in bouncing back from negative emotions. There is no quick fix for any situation, but there is an assurance that you will get better with every experience, and with awareness comes hope if you hold on until life can be taken as a sport. It doesn't require suppressing or avoiding pain or discomfort; passing through it strengthens one. The decision to stay strong comes from the values one stands for and a reason outside them.

Factors Influencing Emotional Resilience

Many aspects influence the development of emotional resilience in a person. Personality traits, both innate and acquired, contribute in a significant way. Some of those factors can be listed below.

1. Awareness / Perspective / Right Thinking
2. Strong Purpose/Optimism/ Sacrifice in Life
3. Detachment/Non-Reaction/Mindfulness/ Spirituality/Humor Sense
4. Will power/ Self Discipline/Selfcare and Assertiveness
5. Connection/Support System/Interpersonal Skills
6. Attitude of Service/ Creativity/Experience

In the subsequent chapters, we will delve into each factor in detail.

Emotional Resilience with Awareness/Perspective /Right Thinking

Demi was famous at her school and had many Instagram followers. One day, her classmates received devastating news: she had committed suicide. According to her parents, she had become agitated due to critical comments from her friends on her posts. Her mother had previously tried to correct her behavior and advised her to spend less time on social media.

Why did Demi take her life? At that moment, she felt overwhelmed and believed her challenges were insurmountable. She couldn't bear the pain any longer and saw no way out. Did she settle for less in life? It's difficult to say definitively, but the intense emotional distress she experienced led her to believe she had no other options.

She needed more ideas and believed she was smaller than the problem. She failed to realize that she was more significant than her problem. How much more could she have achieved if she had been open-minded and had many more important things to pursue? She was courageous but could have applied it for the right reasons. Challenges in life are, therefore, learning opportunities.

"All learning begins when our comfortable ideas turn out to be inadequate." - **John Dewey.**

I heard that human life is precious from childhood, but I have yet to grasp its meaning truly. However, considering it in the context of evolution sheds light on its significance. Let's take the example of a plant: it cannot move from where the seed sprouted and rooted, right? It has to survive with what is available within its reach. If no water is nearby, it can't move to get water and can only stretch its roots to the maximum possible. That's probably why desert plants started storing water in their leaves, like cacti.

Now, let's compare ourselves with plants. Can we walk? Talk? Think? Act? How was it made possible? We evolved from lower life forms. We are the results of their deepest desires and their challenges. Should we value our existence? We could relate better if we got into a time machine and experienced life as plants or lower forms of animals. So, it becomes clear that evolution needs pain and challenge - your memory is associated with your deepest emotions.

"To live is to suffer, to suffer is to find some meaning in suffering." - **Friedrich Nietzsche.**

What if your challenges are the paths you should follow to discover meaning and purpose in your life? As you face and overcome these challenges, you emerge as a winner and an expert in problem-solving. You become a specialist in tackling these issues, and this expertise holds immense potential for teaching and helping others. Life presents us with opportunities in the form of challenges, but are we missing those chances? Is it because we give up our battles too early? One reason might be our lack of emotional resilience or mental toughness.

Negative Emotions

A negative emotion, as described by Eckhart Tolle, is a toxic state that disrupts the body's balance and harmony. Fear, anxiety, anger, and jealousy interfere with the energy flow, affecting the heart, immune system, and hormones. Mainstream medicine acknowledges the link between negative emotions and physical health. Tolle highlights that such feelings harm your body and impact others, triggering a chain reaction. Together, these collectively form what Tolle terms "unhappiness." Positive emotions can strengthen the body and the immune system, but they differ from ego-generated emotions. Ego-driven positive feelings can quickly shift to their opposites. In contrast, Tolle suggests that deeper, egoless emotions, rooted in your connection to Being, such as love and joy, strengthen the body and immune system without the rapid shifts seen in ego-generated emotions.

Eckhart Tolle encourages us to say, "I feel angry," instead of "I am angry." This indicates you are not the same as your emotion, which is supposed to pass through you. Without this awareness, you don't have emotions; emotions have you. Emotional thoughts are energy formations in you based on your mental conditioning.

Emotional Setbacks

An emotional setback is a significant and often distressing disruption in an individual's emotional well-being and psychological equilibrium resulting from various adverse experiences, circumstances, or internal processes. These setbacks can lead to sadness, anxiety, diminished self-esteem, and hindered personal growth. Here are some examples of emotional setbacks that individuals might experience:

1. Academic letdown: Poor grades or exam failure lead to frustration and self-doubt.
2. Job loss: Unemployment brings insecurity, financial stress, and purposelessness.
3. Breakup agony: Romantic split causes heartache, loneliness, and self-esteem to drop.
4. Betrayal hurt: Trust breach leads to anger, sadness, and shattered confidence.
5. Health woes: Illness triggers distress, anxiety, and helplessness.
6. Loss of a loved one: Death results in grief, sorrow, and mourning.
7. Money struggles: Financial hardship induces stress, anxiety, and instability.
8. Rejection pain: Being denied causes inadequacy and disappointment.
9. Public shame: Humiliation leads to guilt, self-consciousness, and social fear.

10. Personal failure: Goal non-achievement sparks self-criticism and frustration.
11. Injury trauma: Physical harm causes pain, trauma, and distress.
12. Family conflict: Dysfunction leads to stress, anxiety, and isolation.
13. Natural disasters: Surviving calamities causes trauma, fear, and vulnerability.
14. Bullying: Harassment results in powerlessness, anxiety, and low self-esteem.
15. Identity struggles: Challenges lead to confusion, isolation, and discrimination.

"Manjhi – The Mountain Man" (2015) chronicles the story of Dashrath Manjhi, a destitute laborer from Bihar, India. When his wife tragically dies due to the lack of accessible medical help caused by a formidable hill, Manjhi resolves to create a path through it. Armed with just a hammer and chisel, he dedicates 22 years to carving a 110-meter-long, 9.1-meter-wide passage, defying all odds.

What made him initiate and complete such a humongous task? Was he getting paid for that? Was he benefiting from that? He thought no one else should endure such a situation and pain as he had. He not only survived, but his life also impacted many others.

Relevance of Emotional Resilience

Emotional resilience is highly relevant today due to modern life's complex and rapidly changing nature.

Emotional resilience is crucial in helping individuals navigate and cope with various uncertain situations, stressors, and challenges. Here's why emotional resilience is critical today:

1. Increased Stress and Uncertainty: Modern life's fast-paced, interconnected nature often increases stress levels and uncertainty. Emotional resilience equips individuals to adapt, bounce back from setbacks, and effectively manage stressors.
2. Mental Health Challenges: The prevalence of mental health issues, such as anxiety and depression, has risen significantly. Emotional resilience can act as a protective factor against the development of these conditions and support better mental well-being.
3. Digital Age and Social Media: The advent of technology and social media has brought about new challenges, including cyberbullying, online harassment, and constant comparison. Emotional resilience helps individuals maintain a healthy self-concept and cope with the negative aspects of digital interactions.
4. Workplace Demands: The modern workplace often involves high levels of competition, long working hours, and changing job demands. Emotional resilience enables individuals to manage work-

related stress, adapt to new challenges, and maintain a work-life balance.

5. Global Crises and Disasters: Natural disasters, pandemics, and other global crises can profoundly impact emotional well-being. Emotional resilience assists individuals in coping with trauma, grief, and uncertainty during such events.

6. Cultural and Social Diversity: Today's world is more diverse and interconnected. Emotional resilience helps individuals navigate cultural differences, embrace diversity, and build meaningful relationships.

7. Personal Relationships: Complex interpersonal dynamics, including conflicts, breakups, and family issues, are common. Emotional resilience enables individuals to communicate effectively, manage disputes, and maintain healthy relationships.

8. Pressure to Succeed: Societal expectations for success and achievement can lead to intense pressure. Emotional resilience supports individuals in setting realistic goals, handling failures, and maintaining a positive self-image.

9. Environmental Concerns: Environmental challenges like climate change can evoke helplessness and anxiety. Emotional resilience empowers individuals to channel their concerns into constructive actions and maintain hope.

10. Life Transitions: Transitions in life (relocating, embarking on a fresh career, or embracing parenthood) blend excitement with stress. Emotional resilience empowers people to navigate these shifts, effectively handling the emotions that come with them.

Resilience Check

Reflect on a recent change in your daily routine due to the pandemic. How did you manage your emotions during this adjustment? Reflect on your ability to find positives amidst challenges.

2. Struggles with Emotional Imbalance

"Emotions are what make us human. Make us real. The word 'emotion' stands for energy in motion. Be truthful about your emotions, and use your mind and emotions in your favour, and not against you."- Robert T Kiyosaki.

Nicholas James Vujicic, an Australian-American Christian evangelist and motivational speaker of Serbian descent, was born in 1982 with tetra-amelia syndrome, a rare condition resulting in the absence of arms and legs. Despite his challenges, his parents instilled a positive outlook in him. He faced bullying and even attempted suicide but was saved. Vujicic underwent an operation to separate fused toes, allowing him to use them like fingers. He began delivering inspiring talks at 17 and graduated from Griffith University at 21 with a Bachelor of Commerce. Nick, born without arms and legs, transformed his adversity into strength, becoming a motivational speaker, author, and disabilities advocate, spreading messages of hope and resilience. Nick transformed his biggest weakness into his differentiator and fueled his work to spark hope in many.

"Strength does not come from physical capacity. It comes from an indomitable will." - **Mahatma Gandhi.**

It need not always be a physical disability; humans face psychological challenges. Likewise, people differ in physical stamina; people differ in emotional stamina as well. Have you seen the Touch Me Not Plant? Mimosa pudica, or touch-me-not, is a flowering plant with unique leaf movements. Its leaves close in response to touch, light, or shaking. This is energy-consuming for the plant and impacts its photosynthesis. Once we touch it, it recoils fast and will take some time to return to its original state.

"Get back up when you fail, to celebrate behaving like a human - however imperfectly - and fully embrace the pursuit that you've embarked upon." - **Marcus Aurelius.**

People Vulnerable to Frequent Emotional Imbalance

Some people absorb others' feelings, compelling them to go the extra mile to help them. These people struggle to differentiate whether it is their feeling they are trying to address or if they are trying to manage others' feelings. These people need to identify their feelings without mixing the feelings of others. People with intuition and feeling as their primary cognitive functions usually have intense emotional struggles. Often, such people or their families are unaware of these psychological differences, adding to the severity of their situation. There are tests to check the sensitivity of people to various factors.

Highly Sensitive Persons (HSPs) and Empaths

Highly Sensitive Persons and empaths share several common characteristics due to their heightened sensitivity to emotions, stimuli, and the environment. While the terms are often used interchangeably, it's important to remember that not all HSPs may identify as empaths and vice versa. Here are some common characteristics associated with both groups:

1. Heightened Empathy: Both HSPs and empaths have a strong capacity for empathy. They can easily absorb others' emotions and energies and may feel deeply connected to the emotional experiences of those around them.

2. Intense Emotional Responses: HSPs and empaths often experience emotions more intensely than others. They may have heightened reactions to both positive and negative emotions, which can lead to a rich inner emotional life.

3. Sensory Sensitivity: Both groups are more sensitive to external stimuli, including sensory experiences like light, sound, and touch. They may become overwhelmed by sensory input more quickly than individuals with lower sensitivity.

4. Overstimulation: HSPs and empaths are more prone to overstimulation in busy or chaotic environments. They may need more downtime to recover from sensory and emotional overload.

5. Intuitive Insights: Many HSPs and empaths have a strong intuitive sense and may make decisions based on gut feelings or inner knowing.
6. Deep Processing: They process information more deeply and thoroughly, often reflecting on their thoughts and emotions at length.
7. Creativity: Both groups often have a creative and imaginative side. Their heightened sensitivity can contribute to a unique perspective and artistic expression.
8. Strong Connection to Nature: HSPs and empaths often feel a deep connection to nature and may find solace and rejuvenation in natural environments.
9. Need for Self-Care: Both groups require regular self-care practices to maintain emotional balance and prevent burnout due to their sensitivity.
10. Strong Emotional Memory: HSPs and empaths may have vivid and lasting memories of emotional experiences, whether their own or those of others.
11. Nurturing and Supportive: They are often compassionate and supportive individuals drawn to helping and encouraging others.
12. Aversion to Conflict: Both groups may avoid or dislike conflict due to their heightened sensitivity to negative emotions.

It's essential to recognize that not every individual will exhibit all of these characteristics, and the intensity of these traits can vary from person to person.

"My strength did not come from lifting weights. My strength came from lifting myself up every time I was knocked down." - **Bob Moore.**

Emotional Imbalance and Energy

Life is a game of energy. Our emotions and energy are closely related. Emotions are energy in motion. If you are overwhelmed by negative emotions, you may be stressed out in a high-energy scenario or burnt out in a low-energy scenario. But if you have positive emotions, you feel relaxed in a low-energy scenario or excited in a high-energy scenario. Feeding our body and mind with positive energy is thus crucial to maintaining resilience.

"Positive emotional energy is the key to health, happiness, and well-being. The more positive you are, the better your life will be in every area." - **Brian Tracy.**

Emotional Imbalance Based on MBTI Personality Type Cognitive Functions

Primary and shadow cognitive functions drive personality types based on their natural preferences. Emotional imbalance is common in introverted Feeler types (INFPs and INFJs), resulting in an energy drain. The cognitive function Ti - introverted thinking is responsible for accuracy, and Fi - introverted feeling is accountable for valuing or authenticity. Often there will be cognitive function loops like Ni-Ti in INFJs and Fi-Si in INFPs, which are responsible for overthinking. It needs to be balanced by corresponding extraverted functions.

"All suffering is caused by being in the wrong place. If you are unhappy where you are, move." - **Timothy Leary.**

According to Personality Hacker, the car model is suggested for personality growth. Overthinking is because of relying more on introverted cognitive functions. Shifting to an extroverted function will help balance the introverted function. For INFJs, balance Ni with Se - Doing and Ti with Fe - Connecting. For INFPs, balance Fi with Ne – creating or exploring and Si with Te - systemizing or effectiveness. Balancing with extroverted cognitive functions will make introverts instantly feel good.

"Your thoughts determine your frequency, and your feelings tell you immediately what frequency you are on." - **Rhonda Byrne.**

Emotional Imbalance Based on Trauma

In his talk on reframing a challenging moment, Dr. Gabor Maté talks about how we generate responses to situations concerning our conditioned mind. He relates his reaction to his friend being late to his childhood abandonment incident by his mother during World War II. He says our past traumas condition our responses when similar triggers happen, leaving us unable to judge the situation and answer according to the current and present scenarios. He also talks about the importance of good parenting to ensure kids are not traumatized by our behavior and narrates his experience of having ADHD. He says our brain develops as a child based on environmental inputs, and the delicate brain picks up response mechanisms early. He was also narrating an incident as a baby where he was among the Jewish babies who cried inconsolably, a condition which was caused by having tense mothers during the World War II social circumstances.

"The greatest damage done by neglect, trauma, or emotional loss is not the immediate pain they inflict but the long-term distortions they induce in the way a developing child will continue to interpret the world and her situation in it. All too often, these ill-conditioned implicit beliefs become self-fulfilling prophecies in our lives. We create meanings from our unconscious interpretation of early events, and then we forge our present experiences from the meaning we've created. Unwittingly, we write the story of our future from narratives based on the past. Mindful awareness can bring into consciousness those hidden, past-based perspectives so that they no longer frame our worldview. 'Choice begins the moment you disidentify from the mind and its conditioned patterns, the moment you become present. Until you reach that point, you are unconscious.'...In present awareness, we are liberated from the past." – **Gabor Maté.**

Our psychological responses result from our generational trauma responses, which are critical in forming our behaviors. The origin of NPD and passive behaviors are also results of this. With this awareness, we can stop passing the trauma to the next generation by bringing attention to our responses. In case of severe trauma, seeking professional support for effective recovery is always advisable.

"A person with power has control of their emotions. A person with power can stop fear, stop depression, or they can augment a positive emotion." - **Frederick Lenz.**

Emotional Resilience with a Strong Purpose/ Optimism/ Sacrifice in Life

Margaret and Cyril have three kids. Cyril had to travel for his official commitments to London for a month. What Margaret then heard was medical emergency news about the untimely demise of Cyril. It was also informed that completing all formalities would take a month to send his remains to her country. Their younger son, who was three years old, had to join his new school the next day after this news. Margaret was seen taking him to his school and doing the essential formalities of his joining procedure.

What made Margaret rise to the situation? Did she have an immediate purpose? A purpose beyond her pain? She could rise for the love of her children.

"When there is a goal, you feel able to overcome any problems as there's future success waiting for you." - **Alfred Adler.**

Without us knowing, thousands of cells and organs are working to keep us alive. Are we controlling that? We think our body is ours. We are indeed nourishing it. But are we consciously doing the whole job of keeping our bodies alive? No. So we can conclude the role of our unconsciousness, connected events in nature, and a supreme intelligence behind our living. What if nature designed us for a specific cause, and our parents were mere instruments to bring us into this world? So, what's nature's purpose for us? I am sure nobody comes and tells you your life purpose. That needs to be found out ourselves.

"The purpose of life is the life of purpose." - **Robin S. Sharma.**

We saw that our responses to the incidents in life have multiple implications that can lift or put down our energy levels. We keep moving forward by consciously trying to move forward at every instance. Maintaining positive energy levels and having objectives in life make resilience automatic for us.

Resilience Check

Reflect on an instance when a work task didn't go as planned while working remotely. How did you handle potential frustration and stay motivated to find a solution or learn from the experience?

3. Merits of Emotional Independence

"If you cannot control your emotions, you cannot control your money." - Warren Buffett.

Often hailed as a basketball legend, Michael Jordan navigated a journey fraught with hurdles before basking in the glory of triumph. His ascent to greatness was marked by setbacks that could have easily shattered his resolve. Despite early struggles, including being cut from his high school basketball team, Jordan refused to succumb to defeat. He used these setbacks as fuel to propel himself to higher levels of excellence. The pinnacle of his struggles came from playoff defeats, especially against the Detroit Pistons, who seemed to have a stranglehold on his championship aspirations. Jordan's response was not to give in but to push himself beyond limits. He transformed physically and mentally, elevating his game to an unprecedented level.

Finally, in the early 1990s, Jordan and his Chicago Bulls conquered their formidable adversaries, capturing multiple NBA championships. His unwavering dedication and unrelenting work ethic ultimately led to his success, a fitting tribute to his perseverance.

"My attitude is that if you push me towards something that you think is a weakness, then I will turn that perceived weakness into a strength." - **Michael Jordan.**

Often, setbacks or external events or reactions upset us, leading to thoughts about the past. The focus of our thoughts is completely on the causes that led to a disturbance in us, which gradually makes us feel low, indicating that our energy is low. What if I say that investing our time and focus on the past, where we don't have any control, is causing our energy to deplete? We completely forget about what we already have at that time as we focus on what we don't have.

"Let not your mind run on what you lack as much as on what you have already." - **Marcus Aurelius.**

What Jordan did was to let go of what happened to him and move on faster with physical and mental uplift. He used his present moment wisely to build a better self as he was free to select his way forward and use his present moments. He didn't try to alter what happened and was not complaining or bothered about it. He was free from the remarks about what happened to him and how others viewed him. He chose that freedom for himself.

"Freedom is the only worthy goal in life. It is won by disregarding things that lie beyond our control." - **Epictetus.**

Can you recollect some tough times you would have had? You were lying on the bed crying or were sitting alone thinking about all that shouldn't have happened, what you would have done right, etc. Gradually, you moved on to do something else, which took your attention away from that problem. So, you agree that other distractions or responsibilities made you move on.

"The secret of change is to focus all of your energy not on fighting the old, but on building the new." - **Dan Millman.**

Emotional Independence

Emotional independence signifies the liberation of individuals from the shackles of seeking external validation and approval to validate their emotions. It empowers them to autonomously manage and navigate their feelings, detached from the need for constant external affirmation. This self-reliance allows for a healthier emotional state, fostering resilience and self-confidence. By embracing their emotions without solely relying on external sources, individuals can forge a more authentic and internally grounded sense of well-being. Are you Emotionally Independent? Do you bother about others' opinions and allow them to define you?

"I have never met a strong person with an easy past." - **Atticus.**

No one can evoke your emotions without your consent if you know their opinion doesn't define you. Cultivate inner serenity amidst external circumstances. Trust your genuine intentions; you don't always have to explain. Those who are open to you will understand you; those who judge you will judge you anyway. Over time, your transformation will speak volumes. Channel your energy into growth. Perfectionism masks the dread of rejection. No one began flawlessly. Embrace your progress, be self-compassionate, and steadily advance despite uncertainty.

"A woman is like a tea bag - you can't tell how strong she is until you put her in hot water." - **Eleanor Roosevelt.**

This holds for everyone. Unless we are tested, we don't honestly know our strengths. Have you observed engineers testing the tensile strength of steel? Based on its strength, they use it to construct structures requiring proportional strength. What if we are being tested for a greater purpose? The person you are and the person you want to be are separated only by discipline. Your struggle is a test to determine whether you are genuinely committed to your desired life. What you don't change, you choose. If you're content with your current situation, you might not be willing to see your potential for a better future and world. We are interconnected, so external events impact us, making it tougher to maintain emotional balance.

"Evil can only succeed when those who are good do not take action." - **Edward Burke.**

When we say yes to something, we say no to many other things. By cultivating emotional Independence, we conserve our energy for tending to productive areas rather than focusing on areas where we lack control.

Ways to Achieve Emotional Independence

Gaining Independence enhances confidence, reduces reliance on others, lessens stress, and fosters happiness. Financial autonomy leads to freedom and accomplishment. It improves decision-making, personal growth, and creativity and widens horizons, offering more opportunities. Independence heightens self-value and self-esteem, empowering personal success and improved relationships. An article in Psychology Today provides the following factors to achieve emotional Independence:

1. Recognize internal control: Focus on changing from within instead of external circumstances.
2. Self-analysis: Explore your contributions to your world, identify self-defeating behaviors, and question automatic reactions.
3. Evolve internally: Embrace change within yourself rather than solely attempting to alter the external world.
4. Define emotional Independence: Cultivate inner resilience to handle stress and challenges, building from within rather than relying on external factors.
5. Self-awareness: Understand personal triggers and reactions in relationships.
6. Assume responsibility: Acknowledge your role in challenges, taking control of emotions and responses.

7. Understand brain influence: Know that happiness originates from how you perceive experiences, allowing you to control emotions through mindset changes.
8. Embrace change: Open yourself to new experiences and personal growth, relinquishing comfort zones for self-confidence in handling any situation.

The Power of Detachment

As articulated by Deepak Chopra, the Law of Detachment emphasizes the concept of letting go of attachment to outcomes and desires. True fulfillment and inner peace arise when we release our fixation on specific results, allowing life to unfold naturally. By detaching from the need for things to happen in a certain way, we open ourselves to greater possibilities and experience a sense of freedom from the limitations of our expectations. This practice encourages a more relaxed and open-minded approach to life, enabling us to fully navigate challenges with greater ease and embrace the present moment. Do you love yourself? Have you made yourself worthy of your love? No? You will want others to love you. You will continue to attach yourself to others to feel fulfilled. If you love yourself enough, you will invest in nourishing your body and mind. Once you are complete, you will have enough love to give it to others without attaching them.

"Never give from the depths of your well, but from your overflow." – **Rumi**.

The logic of detachment is loving yourself more so that your happiness does not depend on anyone or anything else outside. To attach means we are giving control of our life to others or outside events or objects. So, when those things change, we are automatically affected.

True and pure love encompasses all - it doesn't differentiate. If we are happy with ourselves, we can generate love within ourselves. We will not search for love to become satisfied and fulfilled. It's unwise to find happiness only in some people or by owning objects. It's not sustainable, as everything is temporary in this world. Everything has to change. Life is the pursuit of finding the happiness we seek outside ourselves. Once we can find it within ourselves, we will stop chasing it outside and will be full to share what we have with others without attaching them to us. That's the essence of the word from the Bible, "Love your neighbor as yourself." - **Mark 12:31**.

Mel Robbins paints an intriguing perspective—jealousy is a form of desire, a signal that can guide us toward the very things we admire in others. Imagine this: Marie is drawn to John. Will their connection deepen into something more? Let's explore three scenarios:

1. If John doesn't reciprocate Marie's interest, she might feel disappointed. Yet, she's likely to march forward with her life over time.
2. John and Marie could spark a relationship that flourishes or decide amicably to part ways.

3. If Marie senses a changed John and contemplates ending things, it could bring emotional turmoil to John.

In this dance of possibilities, the undercurrent is "desire," steering the course of relationships. Remarkably, this desire isn't chained to one person; it's not a constant emotion tethered to an individual. Instead, it's often linked to an idea of a person or a situation. As the scene shifts, so do our emotions, reshaping dynamics.

Inspired by Mel Robbins' notion of using jealousy to inspire change, can't we extend this insight to attachment? Imagine if we redirected our attachment energy toward goals or desired scenarios rather than clinging to people. Robbins reminds us—jealousy (desire) often stems from insecurity, fear, or comparison. Similarly, our impulse for attachment and attraction can ignite the pursuit of our ambitions.

It's pivotal to grasp the significance of finding completeness within ourselves. Dependence on others to plug our gaps breeds a cycle of attachment—authentic love blossoms when we're self-sufficient. Thus, we can channel our motivation into personal triumphs by employing jealousy or the desire for attachment as a catalyst. This fills us with more profound contentment and nurtures relationships rooted in authenticity, not dependency.

Liberation arrives when we love without clinging to external reactions. The urge to attach might signal a shortage of self-love or overreliance on external energy. Remarkably, we harbor a sustainable energy source within. Overlooking this leads to perpetual dependence on external energies, a fragile foundation. Interactions are energy exchanges; giving should replenish our reserves, fostering emotional equilibrium. Balancing this energy flow becomes a secret to emotional well-being.

The Power of Non-Reaction

Non-Reaction controls your urge to respond to a provocation based on your emotions. Non-reaction offers stress management and improves relationships. Through practices like diaphragmatic breathing, meditation, and mindfulness, you can respond thoughtfully in situations. Delay reactions to assess circumstances and respond effectively. Meditation enhances awareness of triggers and aligns responses with goals. The "STOP" technique aids in stress and anger management, providing a mindful approach: Stop, Take a breath, Observe, and Proceed. Consistent practice empowers you to choose balanced reactions.

"You can only be in a state of non-reaction if you can recognize someone's behavior as coming from the ego, as being an expression of the collective human dysfunction. When you realize it's not personal, there is no longer a compulsion to react as if it were." - **Eckhart Tolle.**

Emotional Resilience with Detachment/Non-Reaction/Mindfulness/Spirituality/Humor Sense

There is a story in the Bible that indicates the essence of resilience. Once, God tested Abraham, commanding him to sacrifice his beloved son. Though filled with sorrow, Abraham showed unwavering faith, ready to obey. He prepared to carry out the divine order as they reached the appointed place. But just as he was about to do it, an angel halted him, declaring God's approval of his faith. A ram appeared, taking the son's place as a sacrifice. This profound trial showcased Abraham's unyielding devotion, a testament to trust in the divine.

"Your children are not your children. They are the sons and daughters of life's longing for itself. They come through you but not from you, and though they are with you, yet they belong not to you." - **Khalil Gibran.**

This story also shows the requirement of a willing mind to sacrifice what is most beloved for you. Also, it gives lessons on non-attachment and expectations for the outcome of our efforts. Abraham's willingness also shows a love for God and his decisions. His love was unconditional, without selfishness, fear of loss, and need fulfillment. It was a total surrender without any question or revolt. Even though the story is biblical, it's evident that we don't have any control over potential circumstances in our life. These aspects can prepare us and allow changes to happen to us without resistance. If we can find happiness irrespective of conditions, people, or possessions, our resilience will be faster.

"The root of suffering is attachment." - **Buddha.**

We possess what we have as we have paid money and bought it, or we have the talent to create it. What if you could buy or make it since resources were available to buy or make it in the first place? If that thing you wanted to buy was not created or available, could you possess that? So irrespective of your buying ability, somebody made it available for you. Are we not using the talents that can be taken away at any time? Do you own it? Can you keep it forever with you? – That should bring an attitude of gratitude and detachment in us.

"Find a person who has embraced anger, and you will find a person with a wounded ego." - **Dallas Willard**.

Anger is an apparent response to someone or something that displeased us. It is normal to feel anger, but we have a choice to respond or not. Sometimes people intentionally provoke us to ensure we are irritated. Non-response or a reply based on humor will be the best response. Anger is a reaction. Non-reaction does not mean you should not respond. But it advises you to take sufficient time to process your emotions and respond wisely. Your anger can be a catalyst to work on essentials for a befitting response. Sometimes your progress or moving on will be the best response to people who intentionally let you down.

"Humor is almost always anger with its makeup on." - **Stephen King.**

In the movie "Late Night," watching how the TV host Katherine Newbury (Emma Thompson) hires Molly Patel (Mindy Kaling) to revive her show is interesting. Threatened with replacement, Katherine resists, using humor and Molly's fresh ideas to save her career. A scandal is revealed, but Katherine's sincerity and comedic approach win over the audience and network, securing her place.

Humor can get the message across without sounding harsh. It can save relationships and make people respond more calmly. It is also interesting to observe what makes us angry. It says a lot about your tolerance and values, as value violation angers you.

"A man is about as big as the things that make him angry."
- Winston Churchill.

Non-reaction and a sense of humor are thus two aspects that can improve our emotional resilience.

Resilience Check

Reflect on when you felt isolated from loved ones. How did you seek emotional support and maintain connections? Reflect on your capacity to communicate effectively and nurture healthy relationships.

4. Becoming Intelligent with Emotions

"Let's not forget that the little emotions are the great captains of our lives and we obey them without realizing it."- Vincent Van Gogh.

Ellen DeGeneres faced a significant turning point in her career and personal life when she openly acknowledged her sexuality on her television show in 1997. The episode where her character came out as gay marked a groundbreaking moment in media history. While she received praise for her courage, the revelation also led to backlash and even threats to her career. Despite the challenges, Ellen persevered. She returned to success with her sitcom "The Ellen Show" and later achieved remarkable heights with the " Ellen DeGeneres Show." Her humor and relatability allowed her to connect deeply with her audience, using laughter to bridge gaps and uplift spirits. Ellen's journey highlighted the power of authenticity and exemplified the resilience needed to navigate adversity while maintaining one's true self.

If Ellen didn't open up her reality to her audience, fearing a backlash, she would have missed the opportunity of freedom to be who she was and had to hide her identity.

"Sometimes what looks like an obstacle in your path is a gift meant to move you in a different direction." - **Jane Lee Logan.**

Emotions are built, not built-in.

In her TED Talk, Professor Lisa Feldman Barrett shares her Over 25 years of studies on emotions through facial expressions, brain scans, and physiology. In her research, Professor Lisa Feldman Barrett challenges conventional notions of emotions. She emphasizes that emotions are not universally expressed, recognized, or hardwired in the brain. Instead, they are constructed based on predictions made by billions of brain cells working together. These predictions influence how we perceive and react to the world, including the emotions we perceive in others. Barrett argues that we have more control over our emotions than commonly believed, as we can change the ingredients our brain uses to construct emotions by changing our perceptions and attitude. This understanding can lead to emotional intelligence and improved emotional well-being. However, it also comes with the responsibility to shape our experiences and actions for a better emotional life.

"One of the key qualities a leader must possess is the ability to detach from the chaos, mayhem, and emotions in a situation and make good, clear decisions based on what is actually happening." - **Jocko Willink.**

Three Ways to Better Understand Your Emotions

In her article in HBR, Susan David suggests three ways to understand our emotions. Often, we struggle to accurately label our feelings, which can lead to incorrect responses. To enhance emotional understanding:

1. Expand Emotional Vocabulary: Use precise labels for emotions and explore deeper nuances. Identify at least three words to describe your feelings, including positive ones like excitement. This leads to better self-awareness and intention-setting.
2. Gauge Intensity: Instead of basic descriptors, assess emotions on a scale of 1-10, considering depth and urgency. Recognize different levels of emotions, e.g., irritability vs. anger. This aids in tailored responses.
3. Write About Emotions: Writing about emotional experiences increases well-being and insight. Spend 20 minutes reflecting on past emotional episodes. This clarifies feelings and helps gain new perspectives.

These approaches improve emotional agility, aiding interactions with oneself and others. Addressing labeled emotions leads to better coping and learning experiences. The movie "Inside Out" follows 11-year-old Riley's emotional journey as she copes with a move to a new city. Her emotions—Joy, Sadness, Fear, Anger, and Disgust—navigate her experiences from within her mind. The film beautifully illustrates that all emotions are vital, as Joy learns that embracing sadness and discomfort fosters growth. There is an instance in the movie where Joy consults sadness on the right path, and sadness refers to it from its experience. The movie teaches that acknowledging our full emotional range and seeking support are crucial for resilience and understanding. The film conveys that embracing complexity and change while valuing all emotions leads to emotional maturity and well-being.

"In the middle of every difficulty lies opportunity." - **Albert Einstein.**

Premeditatio Malorum

Premeditatio Malorum, the Stoic practice of anticipating adversities, profoundly shapes resilience by fostering a proactive mindset. Envisioning challenges in the light of core emotions like joy, sadness, anger, disgust, and fear enhances its impact. Individuals are better prepared to handle potential hardships by mentally confronting them and responding with composure instead of shock. This practice also dismantles irrational fears, offering a sense of emotional control. Premeditatio Malorum boosts adaptability through scenario rehearsal, enhancing flexibility in thinking and coping strategies. This Stoic tool equips individuals to face and overcome challenges with a poised and composed approach.

For instance, Sarah applies Premeditatio Malorum to her exams, envisioning challenges and emotions. This mental preparation helps her stay composed, manage fears, and adapt, enhancing her resilience during tests.

"If you believe it will work out, you will see opportunities. If you believe it won't, you will see obstacles." - **Wayne Dyer.**

The Theory of Constructed Emotions

This theory proposes that emotions are built by the brain as concepts based on past experiences. Our ability to recognize subtle emotions (emotional granularity) and bodily signals (interoception) allows deliberate control over our emotional responses.

According to an article in Forte labs, we can change our emotions through six practical steps:

1. Experiment with New Views: See a looming deadline as a chance to showcase your skills, not just pressure.
2. Redefine Feelings: Break stress into a fast heartbeat and tense muscles; see it as energy for challenges.
3. Share Emotions: Talk to friends about frustration at work for clarity and support.
4. Move Your Body: Walk off irritability, interrupting negativity with physical activity.
5. Enhance Vocabulary: Specify emotions – "annoyed" or "irate" – for better understanding.
6. Write Experiences: After a tough day, jot down feelings to gain perspective and emotional management.

The theory of Constructed Emotions empowers us to shape our emotional landscape through deliberate actions actively.

"Everything can be taken from a man but one thing: the last of the human freedoms - to choose one's attitude in any given set of circumstances, to choose one's own way." - **Viktor Frankl.**

Strategies for Emotional Intelligence at Work

Emotional intelligence (EQ), introduced by Daniel Goleman, encompasses self-awareness, self-regulation, motivation, empathy, and social skills. EQ assessment helps match roles to workplace emotional strengths, fostering better interaction and productivity. A high EQ facilitates communication, motivation, and teamwork for leadership, promoting a positive environment. EQ complements cognitive intelligence and is crucial for personal growth, effective relationships, and successful leadership.

Daniel Goleman narrates about his High School reunion, where he met one of his classmates who was very average in his studies and IQ but the most successful. He says he is the best person to work with because of his teamwork and excellent people skills. He mentions a method to compare the skills of the star performers in a particular role – competency modeling. He points out EQ as the most important compared to threshold competencies like technical skills. He says the higher you go in any organization, the more emotional intelligence matters for managing people.

Emotional distraction is far more intense than external distraction. He says Emotional Intelligence helps you manage that and encourages you to have an optimistic or growth mindset. EI is a learnable skill. Daniel says Leaders' emotional state is contagious, and that impacts performance. So, managing themselves is part of leadership. According to him, one key aspect of handling emotions is naming the emotion. It is because once a negative emotion is called, the pre-frontal cortex part of the brain takes over, and it is the most powerful part of the brain. So simply by naming or talking about an emotion, we feel far better.

The Science of Romantic Love

Dr. Helen Fisher, a prominent researcher on love, explains that the initial stage of intense romantic love is driven by the oldest part of the brain, which is associated with primal urges and obsession. During this phase, the rational decision-making areas in the brain's prefrontal cortex tend to become less active. As a result, people in this state may overlook certain aspects and idealize their partners.

Dr. Fisher suggests that individuals considering important long-term commitments, like marriage, should spend significant time with their partners. This prolonged interaction diminishes the intense initial romantic feelings, enabling a more realistic perspective to emerge. When the euphoria of early love subsides, people can better assess their partner and the relationship, leading to more informed and stable decisions. This approach minimizes the likelihood of making impulsive decisions driven solely by the intensity of the initial feelings. It increases the chances of making a choice that aligns with a person's genuine compatibility and goals.

Three Methods to manage emotions in the workplace

Daniel Goleman suggests three spot techniques or practices to manage emotions at work.

1. **Breathing exercise**-Inhale as long as you can, hold it, and exhale as long as you can. By doing so, it shifts from sympathetic nervous system arousal to parasympathetic nervous system arousal. This makes a state of relaxation from a state of upset.
2. **Naming emotions**- Naming the specific emotions and talking about them to yourself or others shift the energy from the part of the brain which is feeling it to the part of the brain which manages it.
3. **Mindfulness-** Practice Mindfulness trains the brain and strengthens the part of the brain which manages negative emotions. Hence, you are triggered less often; if triggered, it is less strong, and you recover more quickly. Daniel Goleman defines resilience according to cognitive science as how long it will take you to go from the peak of an

upset to a highly calm situation. The quicker that curve, the more resilient you are. Mindfulness enhances calmness and focus or concentration.

Habits of Emotionally Disciplined Leaders

These are some characteristics and practices for emotional maturity.

1. Composure: Practice mindfulness and deep breathing.
2. Rational Decisions: Analyze pros and cons. Seek advice.
3. Adaptability: Embrace change willingly. Learn from failures.
4. Boundaries, Time Management: Prioritize tasks. Delegate effectively.
5. Respectful Communication: Active listening, empathy.
6. Conflict Transformation: Mediation, understanding perspectives.
7. Open-mindedness: Seek diverse opinions and feedback.
8. Self-Care: Prioritize well-being, exercise, and sleep.
9. Recognize Achievements: Acknowledge efforts, and celebrate wins.
10. Clear Communication: Concise, avoid misunderstandings.
11. Positive Culture: Lead by example, and encourage teamwork.

"Not to feel exasperated, defeated, or despondent because your days aren't packed with wise and moral actions. But to get back up when you fail, to celebrate behaving like a human - however imperfectly - and fully embrace the pursuit that you've embarked on." - **Marcus Aurelius.**

Emotional resilience with Will power/ Self Discipline/ Self Care & Assertiveness

Have you observed trees growing back even after they have been cut completely? The new trees are growing back from sturdy and deep roots. Why? Next to the compound wall near my house, there is a tree which grew back this way after it was cut down by a neighbour, in some logic and wisdom only know to him. Every year while sprucing up near our compound wall, we observed saplings sprouting from the ground. It has been almost ten years since the parent tree was cut, but its roots are still strong, deep, and nurturing.

"Self-Discipline starts with mastery of your thoughts. If you don't control what you think, you can't control what you do." - **Napoleon Hill.**

Now let's imagine ourselves in the place of this tree. Can we come back multiple times after a major setback? It isn't easy. We tend to think about what happened to us and grieve for a long time. Self-victimization can't help. We have to come out of the situation and start working. We have seen people with self-discipline working towards their goals, cutting off distractions. That's because they stop thinking about what happened to them and shift their thoughts to what can be done now. They are more practical. But let's agree; every person differs in the natural ability of effectiveness. So, becoming more disciplined will it make us more resilient? Yes. But it needs practice and perseverance.

"The great victory, which appears so simple today, was the result of a series of small victories that went unnoticed." - **Paulo Coelho.**

Self-care and assertiveness are vital pillars of emotional resilience. Self-care nurtures well-being, while assertiveness establishes healthy boundaries, fostering confidence and reducing stress. Together, they empower individuals to navigate challenges with greater emotional strength.

Resilience Check

Reflect on a situation where you felt overwhelmed by constant exposure to information and news? How did you manage anxiety and distinguish between reliable and misleading sources while staying well-informed?

5. Developing Emotional Agility

"Our emotions need to be as educated as our intellect. It is important to know how to feel, how to respond, and how to let life in so that it can touch you." - Jim Rohn

Helen Keller, who faced deafness and blindness since infancy, defied challenges under the guidance of Anne Sullivan. Learning touch-based communication, like finger-spelling and Braille, Keller achieved remarkable self-expression, becoming an advocate for disability rights. Her breakthrough moment, associating the word "water" with sensation marked her journey toward comprehension. After graduating from Radcliffe College in 1904, she authored influential books, including her autobiography. Despite her sensory limitations, Keller understood emotions through touch and vibrations, conveying her feelings through gestures and facial expressions. Her writing became a powerful outlet, allowing her to describe her thoughts, experiences, and profound emotions. Through inventive approaches, Keller communicated her feelings and thoughts, epitomizing resilience and the ability to connect with others, showcasing her extraordinary capacity to transcend the confines of her physical challenges.

How do you respond to your positive and negative emotions? Do you possess emotional agility?

Emotional Agility

Emotional agility, defined by Dr. Susan David, refers to our capacity to engage with our thoughts and feelings in ways that foster personal growth and authenticity. It contrasts with the notion of perpetual positivity, advocating for embracing the entire spectrum of emotions rather than solely pursuing happiness. This approach enables us to acknowledge both favorable and unfavorable feelings that naturally arise over time. In her TED Talk, Dr. Susan David states that viewing emotions as good or bad, positive or negative is rigid. She says rigidity in the face of complexity is toxic. Higher levels of emotional agility are required for true resilience and thriving. Emotional agility involves accurately labeling emotions without being controlled by them. This approach fosters a meaningful life, impacting workplaces and communities. It involves acknowledging the diversity of emotions for engagement and innovation.

"Sadness gives depth. Happiness gives height. Sadness gives roots. Happiness gives branches. Happiness is like a tree growing into the sky. And sadness is like roots going deep into the womb of the earth. Both are necessary. The higher a tree goes, the deeper it goes simultaneously. The bigger the tree, the bigger its roots. In fact, it is always in proportion. That's its balance." – **Osho.**

Have you encountered insulting situations where you had to move on without responding, despite feeling compelled to react with facts, simply because you considered the relationships at stake and the long-term implications? "Pain and suffering are always inevitable for a large intelligence and a deep heart. The truly great individuals must, I think, experience great sadness on Earth." - **Fyodor Dostoevsky.**

Handling positive emotions is easy, but dealing with negative emotions is always a challenge.

Radical Acceptance of Emotions

In the article "Radical Acceptance Can Prevent Emotional Pain from Turning into Suffering," written by Jenny Taitz, radical acceptance is explored as a method to manage emotional distress and promote well-being. Radical acceptance, practiced in dialectical behavioral therapy, involves fully acknowledging emotional or physical distress in both minor issues and significant challenges. It advocates embracing negative circumstances, leading to improved emotional management and problem-solving. The acronym RAIN is suggested as a guide: Recognize and pause, Allow, Investigate, and Nurture.

By embracing radical acceptance, individuals cultivate mindfulness and experience benefits such as reduced suicidality, substance use, anxiety, chronic pain, and improved relationships and well-being. The article provides five steps for becoming a more accepting person:

1. Scan your mind for judgmental thoughts: Recognize negative thinking patterns and return to the present reality to effectively cope with situations.
2. Honor your emotions: Allow yourself to feel and use them constructively based on reality rather than suppressing them.
3. Release the tension in your face: Modify your facial expression to influence your emotions and promote acceptance positively.
4. Act willingly: Instead of trying to control everything and resisting what's happening, be open to facing reality as it is. Choose to approach it positively and genuinely.
5. Work on your U-turns: Acknowledge the normality of defaulting to adverse reactions and redirect your mind toward acceptance, allowing continuous opportunities to choose freedom.

Radical acceptance is not about resigning to feeling bad but rather adopting an active stance that leads to positive change and personal growth.

"Life does not offer free lessons to anyone. So, when I say life taught me, rest assured that I paid the price." **- Naguib Mahfouz.**

Measuring Emotional Agility and Resilience

"Everything DiSC® Agile EQ™" aids individuals in recognizing their natural mindsets and the importance of

embracing diverse approaches. The framework introduces eight "Agile EQ Mindsets," each valuable based on context:
1. Receptive: Open-mindedness to different perspectives.
2. Composed: Calmness and diplomacy.
3. Objective: Clear and rational thinking.
4. Resolute: Firmness under pressure.
5. Self-assured: Confidence and leadership.
6. Dynamic: Initiative and influence.
7. Outgoing: Building relationships and candid expression.
8. Empathizing: Understanding and support.

Agile EQ emphasizes stepping out of comfort zones and using adaptability for effective problem-solving by selecting optimal mindsets and approaches for unique situations.

CD-RISC and BRS Scales

The Connor-Davidson Resilience Scale (CD-RISC) gauges one's ability to bounce back from stress using authorized versions (2, 10, 25 items). The Brief Resilience Scale (BRS) assesses quick recovery from stress. Both scales offer unique insights into resilience dynamics, aiding coping and growth.

Emotional Agility for Workplace Success

An article from Big Think underscores the importance of nurturing emotional intelligence (EQ) and emotional agility in professional settings. It highlights the financial

and professional benefits of high emotional intelligence. The concept of emotional agility is detailed through four steps:
- "Showing Up" by openly facing emotions.
- "Stepping Out" to react appropriately.
- "Walking Your Why" by aligning with core values.
- "Moving On" by making deliberate changes.

The article also provides steps for developing these attributes. It suggests finding motivation through goals, seeking honest feedback, creating a learning plan, finding support from mentors or colleagues, and practicing consistently. Learning from others through mentorship is emphasized, leveraging mirror neurons that facilitate observational learning. Additionally, the article encourages individuals to step out of their comfort zones, take reasonable risks, and embrace challenges. It emphasizes that avoiding discomfort stifles growth and maturity, urging individuals to overcome the fear of failure or vulnerability.

"Real liberation comes not from glossing over or repressing painful states of feeling, but only from experiencing them fully." - **Carl Jung.**

Emotional Agility for Effective Leadership

An article by Susan David and Christina Congleton in Harvard Business Review emphasizes the significance of emotional agility and emotional intelligence (EI) for effective leadership. It highlights that healthy human

beings have inner thoughts and feelings, both positive and negative, and managing these emotions is crucial. Emotional agility enables leaders to approach their inner experiences mindfully and value-driven rather than being controlled by or suppressing them. The authors provide four practices derived from Acceptance and Commitment Therapy (ACT) to enhance emotional agility:
1. Recognize your patterns to initiate change.
2. Label your thoughts and emotions to examine them objectively.
3. Accept your thoughts and feelings with an open attitude.
4. Act on your values, aligning actions with long-term goals and principles.

While developing emotional agility takes time, those who excel in this skill are better positioned to thrive in the complex and ever-evolving business landscape.

The article also references an Emotional Agility assessment. The link to the Agility Quiz is provided in the reference section of this chapter.

"If you are irritated by every rub, how will you be polished? Live life as if everything is rigged in your favor." – **Rumi.**

Shame Resilience Therapy

Brené Brown's therapy centers around Shame Resilience Theory (SRT), which she developed through extensive research on shame and vulnerability. The therapy focuses

on building resilience against shame constructively by promoting four key elements:
1. Recognizing Shame and Understanding Triggers: Individuals learn to identify the physical and emotional sensations associated with shame and recognize the situations or thoughts that trigger it.
2. Practicing Critical Awareness: This involves understanding the unrealistic societal expectations and messages that fuel shame, helping individuals challenge and reframe these perceptions.
3. Reaching Out: Building connections and sharing experiences with empathetic individuals creates an environment where shame loses its power. Empathy acts as a counterforce to shame.
4. Speaking Shame: Encourages individuals to openly communicate about their feelings of shame, seeking support and understanding from others rather than keeping it hidden.

Brown's therapy aims to help individuals shift from shame (fear, blame, disconnection) toward empathy (courage, compassion, connection). It emphasizes the importance of vulnerability and authenticity in overcoming shame and developing resilience.

"The pain will leave once it has finished teaching you." - **Bruce Lee.**

Resilience in the Face of Harsh Criticism

Resilience in the face of harsh criticism can be cultivated through the "CURE" approach, as outlined by Joseph Grenny in a Harvard Business Review article with the following steps:
1. Collect Yourself by breathing and acknowledging your feelings.
2. Understand the feedback by asking questions and listening.
3. Recover by taking time to reflect before evaluating.
4. Engage by examining the feedback for truth and acknowledging it. Feedback threatens our fundamental psychological needs for safety and worth, causing distress. However, regardless of the delivery, embracing the truth in feedback helps build resilience.

This approach was demonstrated by individuals at The Other Side Academy, who highlighted that constantly confronting the truth helps them grow and find happiness. "What doesn't kill you only makes you stronger." - **Friedrich Nietzsche**

Emotional Resilience with Connection/Support System/Interpersonal Skills

In the movie "A Man Called OTTO," Tom Hanks plays the role of a retiree suffering from depression due to the death of his wife. Every time he attempts suicide, human interventions occur that thwart his efforts. These connections with people make him active in society, and his neighbors make him feel valued. Consequently, he abandons the idea of suicide to offer his service to people seeking his help. Thus, seeking help and giving support are wonderful ways to develop resilience, as these connections aid in recovering from emotional traumas.

"Evidence shows that even having weak social connections in a stressful situation is really good for your health and your ability to handle that situation." - **Jane McGonigal.**

A study reported in Stanford Medicine summarizes the impact of social connection. People who experience a stronger sense of social connectedness tend to have lower levels of anxiety and depression. Additionally, research indicates that they also possess higher self-esteem, greater empathy, and a higher level of trust and cooperation. As a result, others are more likely to trust and cooperate with them in return. This creates a positive feedback loop, contributing to overall well-being in social, emotional, and physical aspects of life.

"If you are distressed by anything external, the pain is not due to the thing itself, but to your estimate of it; and this you have the power to revoke at any moment." - **Marcus Aurelius.**

Psychologist Edith Grotberg emphasizes building resilience through three dimensions:
1. I Have: External support like relationships, structure, rules, and role models.

2. I Am: Developing inner strengths like hope, caring, and self-pride.
3. I Can: Acquiring skills in communication, problem-solving, understanding others, and building relationships.

Resilience Check

Reflect on a moment when you felt distressed about environmental issues. How did you channel these feelings into positive action or cope with eco-anxiety, showcasing your ability to process emotions constructively?

6. Reinforce Healthy Emotions

"**No matter the feelings. You can transform the energy of your emotions into your power. The ability to continue moving when you are feeling scared, fearful or lazy is the sign of true mental strength.**"- Matthew Donnelly.

Diagnosed with autism at a young age, Temple Grandin encountered difficulties due to her unique way of thinking. Overcoming barriers, she revolutionized the livestock industry by designing humane cattle-handling systems, empathizing with the animals' perspectives. Grandin's advocacy for autism awareness led to her TED Talk and bestselling book, shedding light on the condition. Her remarkable journey from facing discrimination to becoming an accomplished animal behavior expert showcases her ability to turn personal struggles into opportunities for positive change, leaving an indelible mark on both autism understanding and animal welfare.

Temple Grandin turned her difficulties into opportunities by channeling her unique strengths, passion for animals, and determination into tangible accomplishments. Her journey is a testament to the power of resilience and self-acceptance in overcoming challenges and making a lasting impact. Temple Grandin's journey also highlights the animal-happiness-healing-success connection. Animals brought solace, easing anxiety for emotional healing, enhancing focus on talents, and leading to remarkable achievements, positively influencing her overall well-being. "Success is not the key to happiness - Happiness is the key to success. If you love what you are doing, you will be successful." - **Albert Schweitzer.**

Energy Frequencies, Emotions, and Healing
The interplay between energy frequencies, emotions, and healing is a captivating aspect of holistic well-being. Emotions, intricate energy patterns, are linked to specific frequencies — joy and love resonate at higher frequencies, while fear and stress vibrate at lower ones. This connection extends to healing, where alternative modalities like sound therapy and energy healing suggest that balancing these frequencies can enhance healing capabilities. While ongoing research delves into this complex relationship, it underscores the dynamic interplay between emotional states, energy frequencies, and the potential for harnessing these forces to facilitate healing and holistic wellness.
"Joy is a very high-frequency current of energy with a great deal of energy content. Somebody who is joyful has a lot of energy." - **Gary Zukav.**

9 Strategies for Lifting Your Mood Immediately:
1. Engage in Physical Activity: Exercise triggers the release of endorphins, often called "feel-good"

hormones. Whether it's a brisk walk, dancing, or any form of physical activity, it can rapidly boost your mood.
2. Connection with Others: Call a friend or a family member for a chat in person or virtually. Meaningful social interactions provide support and belonging, instantly brightening your spirits.
3. Practice Gratitude: Take a brief pause to reflect on the positives in your life. Jot down or mentally acknowledge what you're grateful for — relationships, achievements, or moments of joy. Shifting your focus to gratitude can quickly elevate your outlook.
4. Listen to Uplifting Music: Music can remarkably influence your mood. Reserve a playlist of your favorite songs and melodies that evoke happiness. Sing along or sway to the rhythm to enhance the mood-lifting effect.
5. Engage in a Hobby or Creative Activity: Pursue an activity that pleases or allows you to express your creativity. Whether it's painting, writing, cooking, gardening, or playing an instrument, engaging in these endeavors can immediately uplift your spirits.
6. Practice Mindfulness or Meditation: Dedicate a few minutes to mindfulness or meditation. Concentrate on your breath, observe your thoughts without judgment, and anchor yourself in the present

moment. This practice fosters tranquility and reduces stress.
7. Seek Nature: Spend time outdoors, be it a stroll in a park, relaxing by the beach, or simply enjoying the natural world. Connecting with nature has been scientifically proven to enhance mood and alleviate stress.
8. Assess Alignment with Your Goals: Examine whether the current disturbance aligns with your broader life objectives and growth. Assess if the issue contributes to your journey, helping you maintain a broader perspective.
9. Consume Healthy Food: Fuel your body with nutritious meals that support your well-being. Balancing diets with food rich in nutrients, vitamins, and minerals will positively impact mood and energy.

Remember that these strategies can provide an immediate boost to your mood. If your mood struggles persist or worsen, seeking professional support is always an option.

Tips for Naturally Boosting Energy Levels

Boosting natural energy levels involves various lifestyle changes. Harvard Health Publishing offers a scientifically grounded approach to increasing your energy naturally.

"Positive emotional energy is the key to health, happiness, and well-being. The more positive you are, the better your life will be in every area." - **Brian Tracy.**

While many energy-boosting supplements lack scientific support, these nine natural tips can enhance vitality.
1. Manage Stress: High-stress emotions drain energy. Combat stress through social support, therapy, or relaxation techniques like meditation, yoga, and tai chi.
2. Reduce Workload: Fatigue often results from overwork. Prioritize tasks and seek assistance when needed to lighten your obligations.
3. Exercise Regularly: Physical activity improves sleep quality, increases cellular energy, and raises mood-elevating brain dopamine levels. Vary walking pace for added benefits.
4. Quit Smoking: Smoking causes insomnia, disrupts sleep, and triggers cravings, depleting energy. Overcome addiction for enhanced vitality.
5. Optimize Sleep: Experiment with sleep duration to determine your ideal amount. Gradually adjust bedtime and wake time to achieve restful, adequate sleep.
6. Choose Low-Glycemic Foods: Favor foods with a low glycemic index, like whole grains, fiber-rich vegetables, nuts, and healthy oils. These foods sustain energy levels and prevent post-meal slumps.

7. Moderate Caffeine Intake: Caffeine improves alertness but should be consumed judiciously to avoid insomnia. Limit intake, especially after 2 p.m.
8. Moderate Alcohol: Alcohol's soothing effect can lead to energy slumps. Avoid excessive midday or evening drinking for sustained vitality.
9. Stay Hydrated: Water enhances performance and prevents fatigue. Dehydration manifests as tiredness, so ensure adequate fluid intake.

"All life is energy, and we are transmitting it at every moment. We are all little beaming little signals like radio frequencies, and the world is responding in kind." - **Oprah Winfrey.**

By adopting these nine actionable strategies, you can unleash your innate vitality and thrive with enduring energy, supported by the credibility of one of the world's most respected medical institutions. Physiology profoundly impacts psychology as bodily processes, such as hormones and brain chemistry, directly affect emotions, cognition, behavior, and mental well-being, underscoring the mind-body connection.

10 Ways to Enhance Emotional Resilience

An article from TIME discusses ten ways to enhance emotional resilience, supported by research findings. These strategies are derived from the study of resilient individuals who have faced extreme challenges and still managed to thrive. The following key points are outlined:

1. Be Optimistic: Resilient individuals balance positive outlooks and realistic assessments of challenges. They acknowledge negative information but don't dwell on it. Realistic optimists disengage from unsolvable problems and focus on those they can solve.
2. Face Your Fears: Resilient people confront their fears directly, as avoidance can exacerbate anxiety. Exposure to fear-inducing stimuli in a safe environment helps create new memories that reduce fear responses. Special Forces soldiers adopt a mindset of learning and personal growth when facing terrifying situations.
3. Have A Moral Compass: Resilient individuals possess a strong sense of morality and altruism. They focus on the welfare of others, even in dire circumstances, which strengthens their values during stress and recovery.
4. Practice Spirituality: Spiritual beliefs can provide a significant source of resilience, fostering community and support. Religious activities can offer social connections that contribute to emotional well-being.
5. Get Social Support: Having a support network of friends and loved ones is crucial during difficult times. Social connections release oxytocin, which

reduces stress, and giving and receiving support enhances emotional resilience.
6. Imitate Resilient Role Models: Role models inspire and support during challenging situations. Positive role models exemplify qualities to aspire to, while negative ones showcase what to avoid.
7. Maintain Physical Fitness: Regular exercise contributes to mental and physical resilience. It helps individuals adapt to stress and reduce anxiety by familiarizing the body with stress symptoms.
8. Keep Your Brain Strong: Resilient individuals are lifelong learners, continuously seeking opportunities to enhance their mental fitness. Learning new information and skills fosters positive health outcomes and psychosocial qualities.
9. Be "Cognitively Flexible": Resilient individuals utilize multiple coping strategies to adapt to different stressors. Developing a flexible approach to challenges, including humor, supports emotional resilience.
10. Find Meaning In What You Do: Resilient individuals derive meaning and purpose from their activities, perceiving their work as a calling. This sense of purpose drives them forward during tough times.

The article also mentions the concept of "post-traumatic growth," where individuals who overcome hardships become more robust and better equipped to face future challenges. These strategies provide insights into how individuals can cultivate emotional resilience in adversity.

"Pain is weakness leaving the body." - **Chesty Puller**

The Healing Power of Connection

In today's fast-paced world, the significance of social connection on well-being is often overlooked. Contrary to common knowledge, research reveals that social bonds influence health as profoundly as diet and exercise. Dr. Emma Seppälä emphasizes that strong connections amplify immunity, expedite recovery, and foster longevity. Conversely, loneliness, on the rise, jeopardizes mental, emotional, and physical health. The positive feedback loop of connection cultivates empathy, trust, and cooperation. Understanding this intricate web of human relationships becomes crucial for developing a healthier, more fulfilling life in a society witnessing declining connectedness.

Resilience with an Attitude of Service/Creativity/ and Experience

What if your suffering is teaching you something to share with others?

What if what's happening to us and how we overcome it is exactly what is intended from us to be chosen as a purpose of life so that we can make life easier for others?

"The meaning of life is to find your gift. The purpose of life is to give it away." - **Pablo Picasso**.

We are all different, and we all have unique experiences. Hence, what we offer will be different—experiencing the world from other perspectives matters. Every experience matters. The more intense your struggles are, the more you learn and the more impact you can make on people.

"We all have different gifts, so we all have different ways of saying to the world who we are." - **Fred Rogers.**

So, the next time you are struggling with an emotional problem, ask yourself, is it the most important thing in your life? Do you have something important to do beyond wasting your time on your emotional reaction? If you still think you don't have a purpose beyond yourself, take your pain as your purpose. Whatever you are learning in your life is precisely your purpose, i.e., to serve others with what you have learned.

"Because he himself suffered when he was tempted, he is able to help those who are being tempted." - **Hebrews 2:18**

Have I made it simple for you? So, if your struggles are immense, are you learning them in the most challenging way possible? Do you want others to go through the pain you went through? No? Do you have a purpose now? What is essential to understand is that your struggles are blessings in disguise to teach you something. So that you will have a purpose in life to make your life worthy of living, with this awareness, can you come out of your situation faster? It's the pain that lays the foundation of our purpose in life.

"You can be healed of depression if every day you begin the first thing in the morning to consider how you will bring real joy to someone else." - **Alfred Adler.**

Have you noticed how listening to a song, reading a book, or watching a movie changes our feelings? Something changes within us, and we start thinking and feeling differently.

"Art is to console those who are broken by life." - **Vincent Van Gogh.**

I have in my contacts the mother of an autistic child who used to share her activities with her child as a phone status. She takes him through a series of art & craft works and cooking classes. Occasionally, she shares pictures of him attending community drumming sessions. There are medical studies that report that drumming has a positive impact on autistic kids.

"Future medicine will be the medicine of frequencies." - **Albert Einstein.**

A study led by the Clem Burke Drumming Project, involving the University of Chichester, King's College London, Hartpury, and Essex researchers, discovered that 90 minutes of weekly drumming improved behavior and brain function in autistic adolescents. Over eight weeks, those learning to drum showed decreased hyperactivity, attention deficits, and improved emotional control. Brain scans indicated heightened connectivity in regions related to inhibitory control.

Kerala, also known as "God's Own Country," is a small state in southern India. In 2018, a massive flood in Kerala was unprecedented and unexpected. While flood rescue systems were working tirelessly, the government called upon fishermen to lend a hand in the rescue. They came with their fishing boats and rescued hundreds of stranded people. The fishermen who navigated the sea didn't find the 7-foot water dangerous and were happy to serve needy people.

"The fishermen know that the sea is dangerous and the storm terrible, but they have never found these dangers sufficient reason for remaining ashore." - **Vincent Van Gogh.**

The fishermen don't learn to thrive at sea in a day. It's a skill they learn from their seniors over time. But it's not only the skill that helps them; it's their extraordinary courage to face nature's unseen and unexpected forces. They tap into their energy from a higher source, believing that in the face of mishaps, the sea will favor them, and they will safely reach their destination.

"I hated every minute of training, but I said, 'Don't quit. Suffer now and live the rest of your life as a champion.'" - **Muhammad Ali.**

Holistic Approaches to Emotional Resilience and Well-being

In the pursuit of self-improvement, a tapestry of methodologies provides diverse insights. Cognitive Behavioral Therapy (CBT) encourages positive mental habits; Stoicism fosters resilience through embracing adversity; Inner Child Healing Therapy heals past wounds, while Shadow work confronts suppressed facets for comprehensive growth. The Yin-Yang philosophy harmonizes opposing forces. These pathways converge, empowering individuals with emotional strength, self-awareness, and inner equilibrium. Physical fitness becomes integral to emotional resilience. A fusion of these dimensions cultivates a harmonious, thriving existence.

Resilience Check

Reflect on when you intentionally disconnected from digital devices and social media. How did this break impact your emotional well-being and ability to engage in offline activities, highlighting your adaptability and self-awareness?

Conclusion

This book has unveiled the intricate world of human emotions and resilience, guiding us toward emotional well-being and personal growth. We've learned the art of embracing change, aligning with our intended paths, and nurturing emotional self-sufficiency to navigate life's challenges.

But our journey doesn't end here. We've also discovered the paramount importance of connections and effective communication. Building robust relationships and mastering self-expression is crucial for ongoing growth as we coexist with others and our environment. Emotional resilience isn't a solitary endeavor; it's interwoven with shared experiences and connections that shape us.

Have you heard about emotional contagion? We all have mirror neurons in the brain that mimic the emotions of others. This phenomenon makes our emotions contagious. The forthcoming book will explore this understanding and the collaboration powered by our emotional resilience.

Armed with newfound insights and fortified strength, we embrace connections and effective communication. This journey promises personal growth and strengthens the ties that bind us as we navigate life's mysteries together.

GRAB YOUR FREE GIFT BOOK

MBTI enumerates 16 types of people in the world. Each of us is endowed with different talents, which prove to be the innate strength of our personality. To understand the deeper psychology of your personality type, unique cognitive functions, and integrated personality growth path, visit www.clearcareer.in for a free download – **"Your Personality Strength Report"**

About the Author

Devi Sunny is a bestselling author and mentor who helps young leaders develop their careers and promote inclusion in the workplace. Her books in the Clear Career Inclusive series include "Raising Your Rare Personality," "Upgrade as Futuristic Empaths," and "Onboard as Inclusive Leaders." "Set Smart Boundaries", "Master Mindful No" and "Conquer Key Conflicts" are the other three books in her Fearless Empathy Series. She works with eligible students and aspiring professionals at Clear Career and can be reached at contact@clearcareer.in.

May I ask for a Review

Thank you for taking out time to read this book. Reviews are the essential for any author. I look forward to your feedback and reviews for this book. I welcome your inputs to incorporate in and deliver an even better book in my next attempt in the very near future. Please write to me at:

contact@clearcareer.in

Your support will help me to reach out to more people. Thanks for supporting my work. I'd love to see your review and feel free to contact me for any clarifications.

Preview of Previous Books

Fearless Empathy Series

Book 1 : Set Smart Boundaries

"Want to find the answers to the questions holding you back? *Ask yourself these five questions:*

1. Are you tired of feeling like a pushover in your personal and professional relationships? It's time to take control and set clear boundaries in the workplace.
2. Are you fed up with constantly giving in to others' demands and not standing up for yourself? Let's work on developing assertiveness skills in your personal and professional life.
3. Do you need help communicating your needs and wants confidently and effectively in your personal and professional life? Let's explore ways to improve your assertiveness.
4. Are you feeling drained and unappreciated in your personal and professional relationships? It may be time to take a hard look at how you set and enforce your boundaries.
5. Are you ready to take charge of your life and start living in alignment with your values in your personal and professional life? Let's work on building your assertiveness and boundary-setting skills.

"**Set Smart Boundaries:** is a comprehensive guide for anyone looking to improve their relationships, advance their career, and achieve their goals. **This book provides a specific, measurable, achievable, realistic, and time-bound approach to setting boundaries.**

The natural ability to set boundaries is different for everyone. Certain people must consciously impose it as they cannot set boundaries naturally. In the MBTI 16Personality types, Intuitive & Sensory Feelers, require training in setting limits.

Get ready for an eye-opening adventure as this book takes you on a journey through the subtopics below, unravelling intriguing insights and captivating stories.

1. Why Spot Takers?
2. Definition of Boundaries
3. Who should set boundaries?
4. How to spot takers?
5. Toxic behaviours in people.
6. Why learn mindful giving?
7. Material Boundaries
8. Financial Boundaries
9. Givers & Takers
10. Why start valuing yourself?
11. Social Boundaries
12. Workplace boundaries
13. Religious and Intellectual Boundaries
14. Why should we protect our vibes?
15. Social Media Boundaries
16. How can we create social media boundaries?
17. How to build boundaries with mobile phones?
18. How to build boundaries with online meetings or classes?
19. How can we prevent abuse?
20. Personal Boundaries
21. Cyber Bullying
22. Sexual Boundaries
23. Why Stop being taken for granted?
24. Time-based Boundaries
25. Trauma Response
26. Signs of Poor Boundaries
27. Signs of being taken for granted
28. Traits prone to be taken advantage of
29. How can you stop people from taking advantage of you?
30. Exceptions to SMART Boundaries

This book is packed with practical advice, actionable tips, and real-life examples to help you set the boundaries you need to achieve success and happiness. Whether you're dealing with a demanding boss, a toxic friend, or a controlling partner, "Set Smart Boundaries" provides a step-by-step approach to help you take control of your life, career, and relationships.

Book 2 : Master Mindful No

Are you tired of feeling overwhelmed in a world that never stops demanding your attention?

Ask yourself these five questions:

1. Do you feel like you're constantly distracted and putting other people's needs ahead of your own, even if it means sacrificing your well-being? Let's Identify if you're a people pleaser and break free from this habit, prioritizing your needs for a fulfilling life.
2. Do you struggle with being true to yourself and practicing self-care? Let's discover practical ways to practice real self-care and be more authentic for a more fulfilling life.
3. Are your fears holding you back from achieving your goals and living your best life? Let's explore your concerns and move forward with confidence and purpose.
4. Do you struggle with managing guilt and difficulties when you say "no"? Let's strategize for managing guilt and difficulties that may arise when speaking "no" to maintain healthy relationships and confidence.
5. Have you ever struggled with saying "no" without damaging your relationships or professional reputation? Let's Learn to say "no" positively and effectively, prioritizing our own needs while respecting the needs of others.

"Master Mindful No" offers practical strategies to help you filter distractions, overcome manipulation, and eliminate fear and guilt to succeed in a constantly demanding environment.

The natural ability to say No is different for everyone. Certain people must consciously learn it as they cannot be assertive naturally. In the MBTI 16Personality types, Intuitive & Sensory Feelers require training in prioritizing their needs.

This book takes you through the subtopics below, unraveling intriguing insights and captivating stories.

1. What is Mindfulness?
2. What is Mindful 'No'?
3. What is Distraction?
4. Why are we distracted?
5. Types of Distractions
6. Cost of Distraction
7. Practicing Mindful 'No' with Distractions
8. Root Causes of People Pleasing Behaviour
9. Courage Vs. Warmth
10. Manipulation Definition.
11. Signs of Manipulation
12. Practicing Mindful No with Manipulation.
13. What is Authenticity?
14. Authenticity and Sincerity
15. How to be Authentic?
16. Cost of Authenticity
17. Cons of authenticity at work.
18. Are your values limited?
19. Is fear what is standing in your way?
20. Why do we fake fear?
21. What are the common fake fears? How can we move forward?
22. Signs that you are living in fear
23. Mindfulness to transform fear.
24. Present-day fears of our life
25. Definition of Guilt

26. Shame Vs. Guilt
27. Shaming
28. Overcoming Guilt
29. Managing Guilt at Work
30. Guilt and Shame as Marketing Tools
31. Principles of Positive No
32. Power of Positive No in Negotiations
33. Saying No as a Productivity Hack
34. How to Say Positive No
35. Saying No at Work

With practical exercises, real-life examples, and thought-provoking insights, "Master Mindful No" is the ultimate resource for anyone who wants to learn how to say "no" mindfully, with confidence and purpose. Whether you're struggling with people-pleasing tendencies or feeling overwhelmed by commitments, this book will help you navigate the complexities of modern life and live a more fulfilling, peaceful life.

Book 3: Conquer Key Conflicts

"Do you crave to break free from the relentless cycle of adjustment?"

Ask yourself these five pivotal questions:
1. Are you tired of avoiding conflicts and arguments and ready to develop the courage to face them head-on? Assess your growth values.
2. Are you seeking practical strategies to transform conflicts into opportunities? Uncover opportunities for success.
3. Do you want to understand the benefits of conflicts and learn how to manage them effectively? Navigate for positive outcomes.
4. Are you ready to choose healthy battles and leave your comfort zone? Discover more authentic answers.

5. Do you want constructive confrontation? Foster a positive attitude and deepen relationships.

"Conquer Key Conflicts" offers 7 **Effective Strategies** to Stop Avoiding Arguments, Develop the Courage to Disagree, and Achieve Deserving Results in a Challenging Environment.

The natural ability to face conflicts is different for everyone. Certain people must consciously learn it as they cannot be assertive naturally. In the MBTI 16Personality types, Intuitive & Sensory Feelers require training in prioritizing their needs.

Discover a transformative guide to navigating conflicts with confidence and achieving excellent results. Explore the drawbacks of conflict avoidance, unlock the potential benefits of conflicts, and learn to choose healthy battles. This book takes you through the subtopics below, unraveling intriguing insights with examples.
1. Definition of Conflict
2. Triggers of Conflicts
3. Types of Conflict
4. Personality Types & Values
5. Values of MBTI Types
6. Personal Value Conflicts
7. What is Conflict Avoidance?
8. Signs of Conflict Avoidance
9. Conflict Avoidance or Value imbalance?
10. Values for growth
11. Result of Conflict Avoidance in Organisation.
12. Tips for Overcoming Conflict Avoidance
13. Should we encourage conflicts?
14. Disagreeing at work
15. Advantages of Conflicts at Work
16. Merits of Difficult Conversations
17. Conflict of Interest
18. Examples of Conflict of Interest at Work
19. Differentiating Conflicts

20. Arguments to Avoid
21. Choosing Value Conflicts for Success
22. Supporting the Right People in Conflicts
23. Conflicts and their Roots
24. Effective Confrontation
25. Mindful Confrontation
26. Tips for Constructive Confrontation.
27. Impact of Communication on Conflict Resolution
28. Effective Communication Strategies for Constructive Confrontation.
29. Importance of Active Listening
30. Applications & Benefits of Active Listening
31. Conflict Management Skills
32. Thomas-Kilmann Conflict Mode Instrument
33. Strategies for Value-based Conflict Resolution
34. Systems for Managing Workplace Conflicts
35. The Seven Strategies to Conquer Key Conflicts

From understanding the nature of disputes to **embracing healthy confrontation**, this book takes you on a journey of self-discovery and empowerment. *With practical strategies for resolution, you'll develop the courage to disagree and achieve positive outcomes in any challenging environment.*

Clear Career Inclusive Series

Book 1: Raising Your Rare Personality

Find who you are to be your best!

What is your personality type? Are you the right fit for your career? Who is a rare personality type? This book provides all the answers. Psychology is the scientific study of mind and behavior. Understand how psychology defines your unique type, growth potential, and suitable careers. Myers-Briggs Type Indicator (MBTI), a tool to identify personality typology, classifies people into 16Personalities. You can belong to any one of these 16 personality types based on your psychological preferences. Some personality types are stated as <u>rare personality types</u> as per MBTI. The personality type <u>INFJ</u> has been explored in-depth in this book. The purpose of this book is to show solidarity to who you are, identify suitable careers for all MBTI types, with a focus on the rare personality types.

Key Learnings from the book - Raising Your Rare Personality

Chapter 1 MBTI Personality Types
1. What are MBTI Personality Types?
2. How can you understand your Personality Type?
3. What are the 16Personalities?
4. Who are Rare Personality Types?
5. Who is the Rarest Personality Type?

Chapter 2 MBTI Cognitive Functions
1. What are Cognitive Functions?
2. What are the 8 Cognitive Functions?
3. What is a Primary Cognitive Function?
4. What is a Shadow Cognitive Function?
5. Cognitive Functions of all MBTI Personality Types

Chapter 3 INFJ Primary Cognitive Experiences
1. What are the Primary Cognitive Functions of an INFJ?
2. How does Introverted Intuition behave?
3. How does Extraverted Feeling behave?
4. How does Introverted Thinking behave?
5. How does Extraverted Sensing behave?

Chapter 4 INFJ Shadow Cognitive Experiences
1. What are the Shadow Cognitive functions of an INFJ?
2. How does Extroverted Intuition behave?
3. How does Introverted Feeling behave?
4. How does Extroverted Thinking behave?
5. How does Introverted Sensing behave?

Chapter 5 Rare Personality Types and Growth
1. Growth potential Function of MBTI Personality Types.
2. What are Functional Pairs?

3. How Intuition works in Rare Personality Types?
4. Strength and Weakness of INFJ Personality Types
5. Famous Personalities of all MBTI Rare Personality Types

Chapter 6 Careers for your Personality
1. Functional Pair strength for all Personality Types
2. Careers for Intuitive Feelers
3. Careers for Intuitive Thinkers
4. Careers for Sensory Feelers
5. Careers for Sensory Thinkers

Resources
Free Test links for finding MBTI Personality, Enneagram, Socionics, Big 5, DISC, Holland Code Job Aptitude Test, etc. are included in the book.
"A man's true delight is to do the things he was made for."
– Marcus Aurelius

✓ **Find Yours!**

Book 2: Upgrade as Futuristic Empaths

Find your strength to give your best!

Are you an empath? Do you know what an empathy trap is? How can you transform empathy into a strength and build successful careers?

Empaths have intuitive feelings (owing to the cognitive functional pair "NF" in their personality type) as their psychological preference. Personality types ENFP, ENFJ, INFJ, and INFPs are natural empaths as per the **MBTI Personality types** according to www.16personalities.com and www.Truity.com. Empaths are also called **Idealists & Diplomats. Highly Sensitive People** belong to these MBTI types. To face the realities of the world and to be successful in endeavours which have larger impacts, empaths need to embrace practicality and rise above their personality stereotype or one-sidedness.

Dr.Dario Nardi, Author of the book **Neuroscience of Personality**, suggests transcendence or the individuation process, a term coined by **Carl Jung,** the essence of which is to have an integrated personality growth. Empaths have a larger role to play in this world and most of them are underplaying their natural strength.

By adopting the 5 key steps discussed in this book, anyone, especially empaths can easily find their career paths to success, thereby leaving a positive impact on this world.

Key Learnings from the book - Upgrading as Futuristic Empaths.

Chapter 1 Understanding Empaths

1. Empathic People or Empaths
2. Empathy Dilemma
3. The Value of Empathy
4. Practising Empathy
5. The Empathy Trap
6. Use of Empathy in day-to-day life
7. Empathy and Business
8. Empathy and Leadership

Chapter 2 Finding your Strength

1. Empath's Strength, Weakness & Dilemma
2. Empaths as Employees
3. Clifton Strengths
4. Machiavelli's Dilemma
5. Empath's Choice
6. Empathy as a strength in daily life
7. Fearless Empathy
8. Nurturing Empathy

Chapter 3 Developing Your Profile

1. An Empath's Growth Cognitive Function
2. Moving from One-sidedness to individuation

3. Challenges of One-sidedness for Empaths
4. The Magic Diamond for Integrated/Transcendent Judgement & Perception
5. Preferred Growth of Empaths Cognitive Functions
6. The Spiral Development of Cognitive Functions
7. Using Empathy as a Strength
8. Essentials for Building an Empath's Profile
9. Careers and Majors for Empaths

Chapter 4 Finding Your Market Niche

1. Sustainable Development Goals in Business
2. Future Job Skills
3. Selecting a Career for Empaths
4. Challenges of Workplace Toxicity
5. Future of Jobs for Empaths
6. Empaths and the Gig Economy

Chapter 5 Connecting & Networking

1. The Power of Social Connection
2. Why are we not Connecting?
3. Impact of Networking
4. Managing Digital Distraction

Chapter 6 Creating Opportunities

1. Opportunities for Empathy in Business
2. Opportunities in Sustainability
3. Empathy Revolution

"Objective judgment, now, at this very moment. Unselfish action, now, at this very moment. Willing acceptance — now, at this very moment — of all external events. That's all you need." - Marcus Aurelius

✓ **Find How!**

Book 3: Onboard as Inclusive Leaders

Find Your Potential to Impact the Best!

How Inclusive are you? Are you unconsciously biased?

Do you promote Psychological Safety?

This book will help you find answers and enable you *Onboard as Inclusive Leaders.*

Innovation, financial performance and employee productivity are indispensable for business growth. Inclusion helps in achieving these objectives of business. Diversity in line with inclusion and equity creates a sense of belonging in employees.

This book helps to develop the essential qualities required to be hired as an inclusive leader; ***understand unconscious biases, the importance of psychological safety and how it has an impact on workplace productivity.***

The book also gives you the free test links to understand your MBTI personality type, strength, and Bias Tests (The Implicit Association test - Harvard University)

Key Learnings from the book – Onboard as Inclusive Leaders

Chapter 1 Knowing Inclusion

1. Why do we need Inclusive Leaders?
2. What is an Inclusive Workplace?
3. Features of an Inclusive Workplace
4. Challenges of Inclusive Workplace
5. Merit based Inclusion
6. Who is an inclusive leader?

Chapter 2 Inclusion Gap

1. Facts of Diversity & Inclusion
2. Microaggression
3. Unconscious Bias
4. 16 Unconscious Biases
5. Bias Test (The Implicit Association Test)
6. The Cost of Unconscious Bias

Chapter 3 Inclusion in Practice

1. Inclusion in the workplace
2. Inclusion Strategies at Ingersoll Rand
3. Inclusion Mandate
4. Expectations of Gen Z
5. Disability Inclusion
6. LGBTQ+ Inclusion
7. Six Signature Traits of Inclusive Leaders
8. Risks of Casual Diversity Programs

Chapter 4 Inclusion Participants

1. Types of Inclusion
2. Physical Inclusion
3. Psychological Inclusion
4. Importance of Assertiveness for Empaths at work
5. Empathy and Neuroscience of Personality Types
6. Preparing the Team for Inclusion

Chapter 5 Inclusion Process

1. Inclusion Strategy
2. Psychological safety
3. International Standards for Inclusion Process
4. Inclusive Job Posting
5. Inclusive Hiring
6. DEI Interview Questions
7. Disparate Treatment & Disparate Impact

Chapter 6 Inclusion Measurement

1. Measurement of Inclusion
2. Gartner Inclusion matrix
3. How Inclusive is your leadership?
4. Fundamental Interpersonal Relations Orientation (FIRO®)
5. Empathy & Inclusion Measurement
6. Industry Measurement of Diversity & Inclusion

"If someone can prove me wrong and show me my mistake in any thought or action, I shall gladly change. I seek the truth, which never harmed anyone: the harm is to persist in one's own self-deception and ignorance."
— Marcus Aurelius

We need more inclusive leaders who will consider others in their decisions and that alone can give rise to sustainable development and positive impacts for people and the planet.

✓Find How

Acknowledgement

My gratitude to the readers of my book, for your time and reviews, and to all my well-wishers for your support. I am indebted to all who reached out to me with feedback and input.

I have to start by thanking my family, friends, and classmates for their encouragement, counsel, and good-natured jibes.

Extending my wholehearted gratitude to everyone on the Author Freedom Hub, special thanks to Som Bathla for his vote of confidence and my fellow authors for their unbounded support.

To Anita Jocelyn for her editorial help towards the completion of my book.

I thank my friends and colleagues who helped me with their insights and experiences of their work place inclusion. Your inputs were critical in the completion of this book and helped me gather information to cover this topic in details for my readers.

I am grateful to Mr. Sareej for his efforts towards the beautiful cover design.

In no way at all the least, I am very thankful to my spouse Jo and our son Yakob for helping me out immensely by allowing me space and time to pursue my interests and creating a conducive environment to achieve my goals.

To my mother Prof.Thresiamma Sunny, I am thankful for her unwavering support and inspiration to always deliver my best.

I could not have done it without you all.

References

Chapter 1

1. Emotion - Wikipedia
2. Emotional intelligence - Wikipedia
3. Emotional Intelligence Can Improve Resilience | Psychology Today
4. Emotional Intelligence (verywellmind.com)
5. Emotional Resilience Is a Trait You Can Develop (verywellmind.com)
6. Emotional Intelligence Vs Emotional Agility (linkedin.com)
7. Balancing Negative Emotions | by Eckhart Tolle
8. https://positivepsychology.com/emotional-resilience/
9. What Is Emotional Resilience? (+6 Proven Ways to Build It) (positivepsychology.com)
10. Resilience: Meaning, Types, Causes, and How to Develop It (verywellmind.com)

Chapter 2

1. https://www.idrlabs.com/highly-sensitive-person/test.php
2. https://www.bing.com/videos/riverview/relatedvideo?&q=dr+gabor+matte+quotes+on+emotions+and+feelings&mid=E1FC8830FE123DB20BE3E1FC8

830FE123DB20BE3&FORM=VRDGAR&ajaxhist=0
3. Personality Development Tools: The Car Model — Personality Type and Personal Growth | Personality Hacker
4. INFP Fi-Si Loop: What It Means and How to Break Free - Personality Growth
5. INFJ Ni-Ti Loop: What It Means and How to Break Free - Personality Growth

Chapter 3

1. How to Live an Emotionally Independent Life | Psychology Today
2. 8 Important Reasons Why You Should Be More Independent - Addicted 2 Success
3. Yoga and the Law of Detachment (chopra.com)
4. Practicing the Art of Non-Reaction - LiveWellFlow
5. Mel Robbins - Jealousy is desire! - YouTube

Chapter 4

1. Lisa Feldman Barrett: You aren't at the mercy of your emotions -- your brain creates them | TED Talk
2. How Emotions Are Made: The Theory of Constructed Emotion - Forte Labs

3. 11 Habits Of Emotionally Disciplined Leaders – Journey To Leadership (journeytoleadershipblog.com)
4. Strategies to become more emotional intelligent | Daniel Goleman | WOBI - YouTube
5. https://www.youtube.com/watch?v=7BBDj4_YfkQ&feature=share9
6. The Benefits of Emotional Intelligence (EQ) at Work | Psych Central
7. 3 Ways to Better Understand Your Emotions (hbr.org)
8. https://youtu.be/H4psi-MeJjk

Chapter 5

1. Emotional agility: how to build resilience in times of crisis - Ness Labs
2. Susan David: The gift and power of emotional courage | TED Talk
3. Using Radical Acceptance to Minimize Suffering - The New York Times (nytimes.com)
4. Growing emotional intelligence and agility in the workplace - Big Think
5. Emotional intelligence and emotional agility - discprofiles.com
6. https://hbr.org/2013/11/emotional-agility
7. Quiz (susandavid.com) Emotional Agility Quiz
8. The Art of Resilience | Psychology Today

9. The Connor Davidson + Brief Resilience Scales (positivepsychology.com)
10. Shame Resilience Theory: Advice From Brené Brown (positivepsychology.com)
11. How to Be Resilient in the Face of Harsh Criticism (hbr.org)

Chapter 6

1. Drumming Improves Behavior and Brain Function in Autistic Adolescents - Neuroscience News
2. 10 Ways to Boost Your Emotional Resilience, Backed by Research | TIME
3. Connectedness & Health: The Science of Social Connection - The Center for Compassion and Altruism Research and Education (stanford.edu)

Copyright © 2023 by Devi C.Sunny

All Rights Reserved. No part of this book may be reproduced or used in any manner without the written permission of the copyright owner except for the use of quotations in a book review.

Printed in Great Britain
by Amazon